What Readers Are Saying About
*Every Young Man's Battle*
*by Stephen Arterburn and Fred Stoeker with Mike Yorkey*

"*Every Young Man's Battle* does the best job I have ever seen on the subject of sexual temptation. Once upon a time we lived in a world that didn't talk about secrets, and that world has brought us to the mess we are in today. Young men must have an honest, blunt, and unashamedly Christian look at their sexuality. This book will save thousands of future marriages."

—JIM BURNS, president, YouthBuilders

"I have never read a book as direct and open as *Every Young Man's Battle*. The profound principles communicate the authors' personal experiences and provide the hope that anyone can overcome a day-to-day battle with impure thoughts. *Every Young Man's Battle* helps you see the importance of taking control over your eyes, your mind, and your heart so that you can completely honor God in every facet of your life."

—SCOTT BULLARD, of musical recording group Soul Focus

"It's encouraging to see some real men stand up and sound the alarm to young men. Stephen, Fred, and Mike's courage to tell their stories exposes what has unfortunately become a dirty little secret among men in the church. The battle cry of the day is for men of all ages to live a pure and holy life, and this book will crush Satan's strategy by giving the troops the guts to talk about what has been taboo in the church for so long. The authors' poignant stories paint a picture of battle in which all men can relate and offer hope and camaraderie to win the war."

—TROY VANLIERE, artist/manager (representing NewSong,
Carolyn Arends, Soul Focus, Jadyn Strand, and Glad)

"There has been a gaping void in the search for holiness, and *Every Young Man's Battle* addresses those issues where others have been comfortably silent. If there is even a spark of desire for purity in your life, this book will kindle that fire… It *is* possible to walk in victory, as you will surely find out after reading the Every Man series."

—MATT BUTLER, of musical recording group NewSong

# Stephen Arterburn
# Fred Stoeker with Mike Yorkey

# every young man's battle
**Practical Help** in the Fight for Sexual Purity

# workbook

A Guide for Personal or Group Study

WATERBROOK
PRESS

EVERY YOUNG MAN'S BATTLE WORKBOOK
PUBLISHED BY WATERBROOK PRESS
2375 Telstar Drive, Suite 160
Colorado Springs, Colorado 80920
*A division of Random House, Inc.*

Quotations from *Every Young Man's Battle* © 2002 by Stephen Arterburn, Fred Stoeker, and Mike Yorkey.

All Scripture quotations, unless otherwise indicated, are taken from the *Holy Bible, New International Version*®. NIV®. Copyright © 1973, 1978, 1984 by International Bible Society. Used by permission of Zondervan Publishing House. All rights reserved.

*Italics* in Scripture quotations reflect the authors' added emphasis.

ISBN 1-57856-757-2

Published in association with the literary agency of Alive Communications, Inc., 7680 Goddard Street, Suite 200, Colorado Springs, CO 80920.

Printed in the United States of America
2003—First Edition

10 9 8 7 6 5 4 3 2 1

# contents

# questions you may have about this workbook

**What will the *Every Young Man's Battle Workbook* do for me?**

First, this workbook will assure you that *you are not alone.* In fact, a large majority of Christian men struggle with various degrees of sexual impurity. You'll find that the authors are refreshingly honest about their own battles as they share what God has taught them about standing strong in the face of sexual temptation. Second, you'll be encouraged by a *circle of caring, praying friends standing alongside you* as you study God's incredible design for human sexuality and learn practical ways to live successfully according to God's plan. Third, you'll *grow in spiritual strength* as you learn to rely on the power of the Holy Spirit to help you live in spiritual and sexual integrity, honoring women (and God) in your thoughts, attitudes, and actions.

**Is this workbook enough or do I also need the book *Every Young Man's Battle*?**

Included in each weekly study you'll find a number of excerpts from the book *Every Young Man's Battle,* each one marked at the beginning and end by this symbol: 📖. Nevertheless, several study questions refer to more extensive portions of the book, so you'll derive the greatest personal benefit by reading *Every Young Man's Battle* as you go through this companion workbook. You'll find the appropriate chapters to read listed at the beginning of each weekly study.

**The lessons look long. Do I need to work through everything in each?**
This workbook is designed to promote your thorough exploration of all the material, but you may find it best to focus your time and discussion on some sections and questions more than others.

To help your pacing, we've designed the workbook so it can most easily be used in either an eight-week or twelve-week approach.

- *For the eight-week track,* simply follow the basic organization already set up with the eight different weekly lessons.
- *For the twelve-week track,* the lessons labeled Weeks Two, Five, Six, and Seven can be divided into two parts (you'll see the dividing place marked in the text).

(In addition, of course, you may decide to follow at an even slower pace—whether you're going through the workbook individually or as part of a group.)

Above all, keep in mind that the purpose of this workbook is to help guide you in specific life-applications of the biblical truths taught in *Every Young Man's Battle.* The wide range of questions included in each weekly study is meant to help you approach this practical application from different angles with personal reflection and self-examination. Allowing adequate time to prayerfully reflect on each question will be much more valuable to you than rushing through this workbook.

**How do I bring together a small group to go through this workbook?**
You'll get far more out of this workbook if you're able to go through it with a small group of like-minded guys. And what do you do if you don't know of a group that's going through the workbook? Start a group of your own!

If you show the book *Every Young Man's Battle* and a copy of this companion workbook to young Christian men you know, you'll be surprised at how many indicate interest in joining you to explore this topic together. And it doesn't require a long commitment. The workbook is clearly set up so you can complete one lesson per week and finish in only eight weeks— or if you'd like to proceed at a slower pace, you can follow the instructions provided for covering the content in a twelve-week track.

Your once-per-week meeting could happen in the early morning before school, on a weekday evening, or even on a Saturday morning. You could meet in the basement or den of one of the guys' homes or at the home of your youth leader, in a church classroom, or a college dorm room. Choose a location where your discussion won't be overheard by others, so the guys are comfortable in sharing candidly and freely.

This workbook follows a simple design that's easy to use. First, each guy in the group completes a week's lesson on his own. Then, when you come together that week, you discuss together the group questions provided under the "Every Young Man's TALK" heading. You might want to show the *Every Young Man's Battle Video* the first week to help open up the guys. Of course, if you have time, you can also discuss at length any of the other questions or topics in that week's lesson; we guarantee the guys in your group will find these worth exploring. They're also likely to have plenty of their own related questions for discussion.

It's best if one person is designated as the group's facilitator. If your group is made up of teens, consider asking an older brother or youth group associate to take this role. This person is not a teacher, but simply has the responsibility to keep the discussion moving and to ensure that each guy in the group has an opportunity to fully join in. If you're all in your twenties, it's likely that one guy in the group will be mature enough to lead.

At the beginning, and several times throughout the course, remind the guys of the simple ground rule that *anything shared in the group stays in the group*—everything's confidential, especially considering the sensitive topics addressed in this study. This will help participants feel safer about sharing honestly and openly in an environment of trust.

Finally, we encourage you to allow time for prayer in each meeting—conversational, short-sentence prayers expressed in honesty before God. Be sensitive to the fact that many guys don't feel comfortable praying aloud in front of others; over time and without pressure, as you come to trust one another, this barrier to praying aloud can be overcome.

# where are we?

**This week's reading assignment:**

**Introduction, chapters 1–2 of *Every Young Man's Battle***

*There's a time-honored code that almost every male I've known has followed. I'm positive that my father and my brothers followed what I call the "Sexual Code of Silence." The code states that it's okay to joke about sex or even lie about it, but other than that, it's your solemn duty—as a male—to keep silent whenever a serious discussion about sex takes place.*

—Steve Arterburn, from the introduction to *Every Young Man's Battle*

## EVERY YOUNG MAN'S TRUTH
*(Your Personal Journey into God's Word)*

As you begin this first study, take some time to read and meditate upon the Bible passages below, which have to do with God's awesome love for you. Realize that no matter what your relationship to sexual lust and pornography in the past, it has not changed God's attitude toward you. You are His precious adopted child, loved unconditionally and completely. Your perfect acceptance in the Lord is the key fact to focus on, day by day, as you rely on Him to guide you through every temptation.

When I consider your heavens,
    the work of your fingers,
the moon and the stars,
    which you have set in place,
what is man that you are mindful of him,
    the son of man that you care for him?
You made him a little lower than the heavenly
        beings
    and crowned him with glory and honor.
        (Psalm 8:3-5)

See that you do not look down on one of these little ones. For I tell you that their angels in heaven always see the face of my Father in heaven.

What do you think? If a man owns a hundred sheep, and one of them wanders away, will he not leave the ninety-nine on the hills and go to look for the one that wandered off? And if he finds it, I tell you the truth, he is happier about that one sheep than about the ninety-nine that did not wander off. In the same way your Father in heaven is not willing that any of these little ones should be lost. (Matthew 18:10-14)

Who shall separate us from the love of Christ? Shall trouble or hardship or persecution or famine or nakedness or danger or sword? As it is written:

"For your sake we face death all day long;
    we are considered as sheep to be slaughtered."

No, in all these things we are more than conquerors through him who loved us. For I am convinced that neither death nor life, neither angels nor demons, neither the present nor the future, nor any powers, neither height nor depth, nor anything else in all creation, will be able to separate us from the love of God that is in Christ Jesus our Lord. (Romans 8:35-39)

1. The psalmist tells us how God views his human creatures. What phrase shows you how much God values you—just for being a human being?

2. When Jesus was on earth, He demonstrated His love and gentleness toward children. Have you ever seen yourself as a "little one" in His eyes? When? How could you begin to develop more of a sense of childlike dependence on Jesus?

3. According to the apostle Paul (author of the letter to the Romans), how strong is the love of Christ for you? What modern-day invention or image do you think might symbolize the strength of this love for you?

4. Can your sexual sins separate you from the love of God? Why or why not?

5. Name the most encouraging truth that comes through to you in the scripture passages above. How will you remind yourself of that truth during the coming week?

☑ EVERY YOUNG MAN'S **CHOICE**

*(Questions for Personal Reflection and Examination)*

  📖 Since everyone is determined not to talk about this, or maybe is embarrassed to do so, you probably don't have a clear picture of what healthy sex is all about. In fact, you're probably thinking that some very wonderful things are not normal and that some very normal things are pretty weird. 📖

📖 Like any red-blooded football player, however, I had more than a passing interest in sex. I'd been hooked on *Playboy* centerfolds ever since I found a stack of the magazines beneath my dad's bed when I was in first grade. I also discovered copies of *From Sex to Sexty,* a publication filled with naughty jokes and sexy comic strips. 📖

6. How have you learned about sex so far? Do you believe you have a healthy view of sex? Why or why not?

7. What is your own experience with pornography? Can you relate to Fred's stories about his early exposure to porn? How was your experience like or unlike his? How do you think exposure to pornography influences a young boy's early perspective on sexuality? How do you think continued exposure to pornography influences a young man's perspective?

8. What is your basic attitude toward the theme of this entire book—
that you can be delivered from the habit (or addiction) of lust and
pornography? What do you see in Fred's story so far that gives
you hope?

 EVERY YOUNG MAN'S WALK
*(Your Guide to Personal Application)*

&#x1F4D6; One of the most difficult assignments you'll ever have
is to integrate your sexuality with the emotional, spiritual,
social, and relational person you want to be. Many have the
tendency to see their sexuality as something shamefully separate and distinct from themselves, but that shouldn't be the
case at all. &#x1F4D6;

&#x1F4D6; Within twelve short months, I'd gone from being able to
say no in a secluded camper on a moonlit night to being able
to say yes in any bed on any night. Just one year out of college in California, I found myself with four "steady" girl-
friends simultaneously. I was sleeping with three of them and
was essentially engaged to marry two of them. None knew of
the others. &#x1F4D6;

📖 This was a different experience for me. Oh, I knew who God was and had even prayed on occasion that I wanted Him closer in my life, but nevertheless I'd be right back in bed the following evening with the French graduate student—or one of the others. I never really meant those prayers. Then again, my word never meant much back then, and I knew it. 📖

9. What does Steve mean by integrating your sexuality with the rest of your life? How do you think this would help you in the battle against impure thoughts and sexual temptation? What would be a smart first step for you to begin integrating sexuality with life?

10. Fred talks about his swift increase in sexual behavior—from saying no to being unable to stay out of bed with various girls! What have you noticed about the "mushrooming" effect of lust and sexual sin? How willing are you to stop this chain reaction in your own life? Why do you think it's vital to do so?

11. If you've prayed about this area of your life in the past, how has God answered—or seemed not to answer? Review what was required for Fred to really mean his prayers? What do you think the same change might require of you?

12. In quietness, review what you have written and learned in this week's study. If further thoughts or prayer requests come to your mind and heart, you may want to write them here.

13. What for you was the most meaningful concept or truth in this week's study? What do you believe God wants you to do in response?

14. How would you talk this over with God? Write your response here as a prayer to Him.

## 👥 EVERY YOUNG MAN's TALK

*(Constructive Topics and Questions for Group Discussion)*

### Key Highlights from the Book to Read Aloud and Discuss

📖 It's sad that in the Christian community, where we have access to God's truth, we operate with so many lies and myths about sex. 📖

📖 Melissa looked up at me with a deep sadness in her big brown eyes, the moonlight framing her innocent face. "You know that I'm saving myself for marriage—hopefully ours," she said. "If you push forward with this, I want you to know that I won't stop you. But I will never be able to respect you as much as I do right now, and that would make me very sad for a very long time."

Laying her virginity on the line, she had delivered the ultimate pop quiz. How would I answer? Who did I love most—her or me? 📖

📖 Shocked by the centerfolds? No, I was shocked by my revulsion. *Where in the world did this reaction come from?* I wondered. After all, we're talking Fred Stoeker, the guy who'd memorized the dates when porn magazines hit the local drugstore. The one who skipped class to lust over the pages. The one who *lived* for centerfolds, saving them for last like some sweet dessert. I'd never been repulsed by a centerfold in my life. 📖

## *Discussion Questions*

(Note: If you're meeting in a group, begin your session by raising the issue of "comfort levels." The point is, the topic and themes in this book might be a little difficult to discuss at first. That's only natural; each of you will be a little uneasy in the beginning. Nevertheless, take courage and move forward. The Lord cares about every part of your life, including your sexuality. And sexual lust is best battled with help from other Christian men who can talk and pray together in a spirit of frank and open communication. So begin with prayer, inviting the Holy Sprit to be in your midst and to guide you in your sharing. It will take some guts, but it will be worth your effort!)

A. In the introduction, Steve talked about a friend's son who said, "Dad, I just feel like taking off my clothes and standing in front of a girl naked." Can you understand that statement coming from a twelve-year-old? How might you have stated it—that hormonal rush that kicked in when you hit puberty?

B. This book freely admits that there are many lies and myths about sex in the Christian community. Talk this over. What things would you identify as lies and myths? How have these affected your attitude about sex, lust, and pornography so far?

C. Fred talks about a turning point in his life with his girlfriend Melissa. He had to ask, "Who do I love most—her or me?" Have you BTDT (been there, done that)? What kinds of decisions have you made in the past, and what kind of impact did they make in your life—and in the life of another? How would you like to decide in the future? Why?

D. Fred was eventually amazed at his reaction against porn—the bathroom wallpaper episode. Can you believe this really happened? How do you explain the change in Fred's heart? What does this event say to your own heart right now?

E. Fred talks about the time he couldn't get aroused with an old girlfriend. Why was that such a profound spiritual turning point for him? Have you ever thought of the Holy Spirit working in this practical way? What does this story say to you personally?

F. Fred says: "I immediately fell in love with the Holy Spirit's whisper in my life." What does this mean to you? Can you think of a time when you have "heard the whisper"? When do you need to hear it the most? Share about this in the most practical terms possible.

# oneness and maleness

**This week's reading assignment:**

**chapters 3–6 of *Every Young Man's Battle***

*I recall how the Holy Spirit whispered to me, "This practice can't be tolerated any-more in your life. You are Christ's now, and He loves you." The implication was that continued sexual activity would hurt my intimacy with Christ.*

*When you break His standards, the Lord doesn't reject you, but you can't be as close to Him.… [Yet] this new life in me was moving me His way. I had a desire to be closer to Him. And in order to get closer to Him, I had to be not so close to those women in my life.*

—Fred Stoeker, from chapter 3 of *Every Young Man's Battle*

### EVERY YOUNG MAN'S TRUTH
*(Your Personal Journey into God's Word)*

In your first session, you focused on Bible passages talking about God's great love for you. It is a perfect love that lasts forever because of Christ's eternal work on the cross. The awesome Bible passage below is a reminder that God's love has also given you a special identity as His beloved child. You've been adopted as His own, and this should have a powerful and prac-tical effect on your self-image. In other words, when you are tempted to sin—remember who you are! When you are tempted and fail to resist— remember who you are! Ask for God's forgiveness, and move ahead in the power of His never-ending love.

> Praise be to the God and Father of our Lord Jesus Christ, who has blessed us in the heavenly realms with every spiritual blessing in Christ. For he chose us in him before the creation of the world to be holy and blameless in his sight. In love he predestined us to be adopted as his sons through Jesus Christ, in accordance with his pleasure and will—to the praise of his glorious grace, which he has freely given us in the One he loves. In him we have redemption through his blood, the forgiveness of sins, in accordance with the riches of God's grace that he lavished on us with all wisdom and understanding. And he made known to us the mystery of his will according to his good pleasure, which he purposed in Christ, to be put into effect when the times will have reached their fulfillment—to bring all things in heaven and on earth together under one head, even Christ.
>
> In him we were also chosen, having been predestined according to the plan of him who works out everything in conformity with the purpose of his will, in order that we, who were the first to hope in Christ, might be for the praise of his glory. (Ephesians 1:3-12)

1. According to this passage, God chose you—but for what purpose?

2. What is your identity in Christ? Let this identity seep into your soul right now. How does it feel?

3. In what types of situations are you most likely to forget about your identity in Christ and all the spiritual blessings that come with it? Why do you think this happens?

4. When you are in the midst of temptation, how could recalling the truths of this scripture passage help you? What one sentence or phrase stands out to you with the most personal impact?

☑ EVERY YOUNG MAN'S **CHOICE**

*(Questions for Personal Reflection and Examination, Chapters 3 and 4)*

📖 Regardless of where you stand right now, let me use my story as a starting point to lay a foundation for the rest of this book. It's an underpinning of six basic truths upon which we all need to agree. 📖

📖 As young men we often treat ourselves as kids. If we viewed ourselves as men like God does, we'd always view our sexual decisions today as having an impact on our tomorrows. But we usually don't do that. There remains this huge gap between the *physical* ability to do sexual things (which happens during puberty) and the *legal* ability to do sexual things (at least in God's eyes), which is ours only at marriage. Facing this enormous chasm, it's easy to view the physical and the legal as two thoroughly separate realms. 📖

5. Go back to chapter 3 and review the six basic truths about sex and your spiritual life. Which of them reveals new information to you? Which of them would you like to learn more about? Why?

6. Think about how you would describe the idea of bifurcation to another guy. Why is it considered a myth? What are some of its destructive effects on young men? On you personally?

### EVERY YOUNG MAN'S WALK
*(Your Guide to Personal Application, Chapters 3 and 4)*

> 📖 If you don't ram a stake into the ground and declare, "This is as far as I go, and I won't go any further," then you'll lose your footing on the slippery slope of sex. Remember how I let myself go in college? Because of the pleasure, sexual escalation was natural. 📖

> 📖 Maybe you aren't concerned. Maybe you think God will forgive you and that everything will be over once you marry. He'll forgive you, all right, but it's not over. Sin comes with inescapable consequences that follow you. You'll have to pay the price at the same toll bridge as the rest of us. Jim told us this… 📖

7. What is your experience during the past year with sexual escalation? Do you agree that it is a slippery slope?

8. What are you currently doing to "ram a stake into the ground"?

9. If God has forgiven you through Christ, then why should you be concerned about sin in your life?

10. What might be some of the consequences of sexual sin that the authors speak about? What price(s) at the "toll bridge" could you imagine having to pay someday?

11. Think about the case of Jim, who was sexually active since he was twelve (now in his late twenties). How did his young-teen actions contribute to his struggles as an adult? Do you see any similar patterns in your own life?

12. What for you was the most meaningful concept or truth in chapters 3 and 4? What do you believe God wants you to do in response to this week's study?

13. How would you talk this over with God? Write your response here as a prayer to Him.

### EVERY YOUNG MAN'S TALK

*(Constructive Topics and Questions for Group Discussion, Chapters 3 and 4)*

### *Key Highlights from the Book to Read Aloud and Discuss*

> When I was fourteen, my sister's boyfriend, Brock, said to me with a wicked little grin, "Once you taste the candy, you'll never say no again. So you better not taste it!"
>
> Brock was right. Once you travel down the freeway of premarital sex, you can't back up. If you want your purity back, then you'll have to exit that freeway entirely.

> Let's go to the source and check out what the Bible has to say on the subject of sexual impurity. Did you know that in nearly every book of the New Testament we're commanded to avoid sexual impurity? Here's a selection of passages that teach God's concern for our sexual purity…

> Like Pinocchio, maybe you think Adventure Island will bring you great amusement at no charge, although you know you're not supposed to go there. But there *will* be a price to pay at the end of the day, and it will be a heavy one.

## Discussion Questions for Chapters 3 and 4

A. Which parts of chapters 3 and 4 were most helpful or encouraging to you, and why?

B. Go back to the beginning paragraphs of chapter 3. Would you say that you are most like Tyler, Brad, John, or the good kid at church? Explain your response to the other guys in the group.

C. Think about Brock's statement for a moment. If you've "tasted the candy," do you agree that you can't back up? What, in practical terms, does it mean to "exit the freeway"?

D. Together, review the Bible passages presented toward the end of chapter 3. Pick your favorite—the scripture that means the most to you right now—and share why it has such an impact on you.

E. Talk about the experience of Pinocchio as described in chapter 4. As you feel comfortable doing so, tell about any kinds of "prices" you may have had to pay for sexual sin in your life. (Perhaps it's just a feeling of guilt or lowered self-esteem. Talk about it!)

F. The second half of chapter 4 reveals the fact that even marriage is no sexual nirvana. Does this surprise you? What practical application(s) for young men do you find in this truth?

---

*Note: If you're following a twelve-week track,*
*save the rest of this lesson for the next session.*
*If you are on an eight-week track, keep going.*

---

## ☑ EVERY YOUNG MAN'S CHOICE

*(Questions for Personal Reflection and Examination, Chapters 5 and 6)*

> 📖 Something was gripping me, something relentless, something I couldn't shake. And my friendship with Christ? Our relationship had changed. He hadn't changed, but I had. I had stopped short of His standard, and I had stopped moving closer into intimacy. I'd said no in my spirit too often, and that stopped the flow of His inner power. I was in bondage. 📖

> 📖 Our very maleness—and three male tendencies in particular—represents the second main reason (in addition to "stopping short") for the pervasiveness of sexual impurity among men. 📖

14. Can you relate to Fred's description of bondage to sexual sin? Think about your own experience: What forms of no have you said to the Spirit in the past? What kinds of yes would you like to be saying instead?

15. Review the three male tendencies outlined in chapter 6. Reflect on how you have experienced these in your own life. Also consider: How have you been receiving sexual gratification through your eyes lately?

### Every Young Man's WALK

*(Your Guide to Personal Application, Chapters 5 and 6)*

So often there's no challenging voice calling us to obedience and authenticity. Instead, we move nearer our peers, often sitting together on the middle ground, a good distance from God. When challenged by His higher standards, we're comforted that we don't look too different from other Christians around us. Trouble is, as we've seen, we don't look much different from non-Christians either.

Your "addictive behaviors" are not rooted in some deep, dark, shadowy mental maze or weakness. Rather, they're based on pleasure highs that enter through the eyes. Men receive a chemical high from sexually charged images when a hormone called epinephrine is secreted into the bloodstream. This locks into the memory whatever stimulus is present at the time of the emotional excitement.

Therefore, our "mind's eye" can cause the same chemical high through fantasy.

16. Who is challenging you to obedience these days? How hard or easy is it for you to respond to God's higher standard?

17. Have you ever thought that your repeated misbehaviors meant there was something "deep, dark, and shadowy" about you? According to the authors, what is the basic message that goes against this idea? What is the status of your "mind's eye" lately? Is it doing what you want it to do?

18. What is the difference between maleness and manhood? Which are you choosing?

19. What for you was the most meaningful concept or truth in chapters 5 and 6? What do you believe God wants you to do in response to this week's study?

20. How would you talk this over with God? Write your response here as a prayer to Him.

## ☺☻ EVERY YOUNG MAN'S TALK

*(Constructive Topics and Questions for Group Discussion, Chapters 5 and 6)*

### Key Highlights from the Book to Read Aloud and Discuss

📖 When I confided in a close friend, he replied, "Oh, come on! Nobody can control his eyes and mind, for heaven's sakes! God loves you! It must be something else." But I knew differently.

I finally made the connection between my sexual immorality and my distance from God. Having eliminated the visible adulteries and pornography, and having avoided physical adultery, I looked pure on the outside to everyone else. But to God, I had stopped short.... I'd merely found a comfortable middle ground somewhere between paganism and obedience to God's standard. 📖

📖 So...are you being authentic? I once asked Thomas, a youth pastor, to describe the level of authenticity he saw within his young flock.

"Not much," was his terse reply.

I asked him to expound. "They seem to have great intentions," he noted. "They desire to be used by God. Trouble is, they won't step out. When I ask them, 'Why aren't you hungrier for God?' I know the answer already. They don't want to stand out. They don't want to put out the effort. They just want to be accepted." 📖

📖 Prayer alone is often not enough for total victory. We can go to the altar of prayer and be freed, but if we stop short and never fully close the gates of our eyes to sensual pollution, the sewage seeps right back in, day in and day out. The chemical highs return, and we're captured again.

So while we're to pray about sexual sin on the *spiritual* front, we have our orders on the *physical* battlefront as well. 📖

## Discussion Questions for Chapters 5 and 6

G. How can you tell if you are stopping short of God's standard for sexual purity? What does this mean for you in practical terms?

H. How hard would it be for you to stand out in your youth or other type of group at church? Why? Is being authentic worth the potential rejection by your peers?

I. Do you agree that prayer alone will not keep you from sexual sin? What else is needed? Why?

J. Look again at the case of Kerry, described toward the end of chapter 6. If he were your best friend, what would be your advice to him?

K. What does it mean for a guy to pursue manhood over maleness? What encouragement or support can your group members give each other? List some practical actions you are willing to commit to together.

# choosing authentic manhood

**This week's reading assignment:**

**chapters 7–8 of** *Every Young Man's Battle*

*"How long will you be unclean?" (Jeremiah 13:27). That's the question for you as well: How long will you choose to be sexually unclean? How long will you keep shutting down the new life within you?*

*We've seen what God expects.... We've seen it can be done. Jesus and Job were authentic men, and they didn't mix standards even when their lives were on the line. Are you God's man, hearing the Word and doing it? If you want to turn things around, authenticity with God is the place to start.*

*—from chapter 7 of* Every Young Man's Battle

## EVERY YOUNG MAN'S TRUTH
*(Your Personal Journey into God's Word)*

Before you jump into this study, take some time with your Bible. Below you'll find three passages of scripture that speak directly of God's will for your sexuality. Basically, they say: *Stay pure!* This can't be accomplished by sheer willpower, however. Read carefully and with an open heart. Ask the Lord to show you exactly what it means for you to rely on His strength in the challenge to live each day in a way that pleases Him. Be assured: He *will* answer and reward your commitment to purity.

> Blessed are they whose ways are blameless,
>> who walk according to the law of the LORD.
> Blessed are they who keep his statutes
>> and seek him with all their heart.
> They do nothing wrong;
>> they walk in his ways.
> How can a young man keep his way pure?…
>> By living according to your word. (Psalm 119:1-3,9)

> Among you there must not be even a hint of sexual immorality, or of any kind of impurity, or of greed, because these are improper for God's holy people. Nor should there be obscenity, foolish talk or coarse joking, which are out of place, but rather thanksgiving. For of this you can be sure: No immoral, impure or greedy person—such a man is an idolater—has any inheritance in the kingdom of Christ and of God. Let no one deceive you with empty words, for because of such things God's wrath comes on those who are disobedient.… Be very careful, then, how you live—not as unwise but as wise. (Ephesians 5:3-6,15)

> It is God's will that you should be sanctified: that you should avoid sexual immorality; that each of you should learn to control his own body in a way that is holy and honorable, not in passionate lust like the heathen, who do not know God.… For God did not call us to be impure, but to live a holy life. (1 Thessalonians 4:3-5,7)

1. According to the psalmist, how can a young man stay pure? What would this look like in your life?

2. In Ephesians, the apostle Paul went into detail about the things a Christian is to avoid. Make your own list of contemporary things to avoid, based upon this passage. Ask the Lord to keep you free from each item.

3. The word *sanctified* means to be dedicated for God's use. Since God's will is that you be sanctified, what changes might be needed in your daily lifestyle?

4. Think about what living a sanctified life would be like—and then prayerfully invite the Spirit of God to help you live it!

☑ EVERY YOUNG MAN'S CHOICE
*(Questions for Personal Reflection and Examination)*

📖 Don't be discouraged. Instead, learn from Job.

First, we need to learn more about how Job did it. In Job 31:1, we see Job making this startling revelation: "I made a covenant with my eyes not to look lustfully at a girl." A covenant with his eyes! You mean he made a promise with his eyes to not gaze upon a young woman? 📖

📖 If you aren't trustworthy in handling fleshly passions, how can you be trusted to handle things of greater value? Jesus said that if you were faithful in the little things, He would entrust you with bigger things. In this, God isn't primarily referring to what He's called you to *do* in His kingdom. He's primarily concerned with what He's called you to *be* in your character. 📖

5. How does the idea of a covenant with your eyes strike you? Do you think you could make this kind of covenant before God?

6. What is the difference between seeing and gazing? What specific steps should we commit to ahead of time, in order to prevent one from becoming the other?

7. Think through the distinction between what you do and what you are. Why is your growth in character so important to the Lord?

### 🥾 EVERY YOUNG MAN'S WALK
*(Your Guide to Personal Application)*

📖 "Oh, don't be so hard on yourself," you might say. "It's natural for guys to look. That's part of our nature." But what you're doing is stealing. The impure thought life is the life of a thief. You're stealing images that aren't yours. 📖

📖 A few years back, Cyndi was known throughout her church as a girl who lived purely and radically for God, a high school student with high standards. I'll never forget a conversation I had with her. "Is it hard to hold such high standards like you do?" I asked.

"Oh, I don't mind being mocked," she replied. "Christ was mocked plenty. That's just part of it." 📖

    📖 At Calvary, He purchased for you the freedom and
authority to live in purity. That freedom and authority are
His gifts to you through the presence of His Spirit, who took
up residence within you when you gave your life to Christ.
The freedom and authority are wrapped up in our new inner
connection to His divine nature, which is the link that gives
us His power and the fulfillment of His promises. 📖

8. Explain the logic behind the idea that looking is actually stealing. Do you agree or disagree? During the past week, have you been a thief in this manner?

9. What is your attitude toward someone like Cyndi? Do you respect her? Why or why not?

10. How would you describe to a non-Christian what Christ's death means to you? How does what happened at Calvary make a difference in how you will act today and tomorrow?

11. Think on the story of high school sophomore Ben (chapter 8). He came to the conclusion that he hadn't yet reached the point of hating his sin. Honestly consider: "Is that where I am too?"

12. In quietness, review what you have written and learned in this week's study. If further thoughts or prayer requests come to your mind and heart, you may want to write them here.

13. What for you was the most meaningful concept or truth in this week's study? What do you believe God wants you to do in response?

14. How would you talk this over with God? Write your response here as a prayer to Him.

## EVERY YOUNG MAN'S TALK

*(Constructive Topics and Questions for Group Discussion)*

### Key Highlights from the Book to Read Aloud and Discuss

📖 You may be thinking, *Who in their right mind would ever make a covenant with his eyes like this? It seems crazy.* What I did on Merle Hay Road may seem odd to you. But remember, acts of obedience often appear strange, even illogical. 📖

📖 Have you had it with the running? In his early twenties, author and pastor Jack Hayford once sat in his car after a banking transaction with a lovely bank teller and said to himself, "I'm either going to have to purify my mind and consecrate myself unto God, or I'm going to have to masturbate right here." That Jack could say this in front of tens of thousands of men at a Promise Keepers conference was inspirational. How about you? 📖

📖 Each one of us has been manipulated by our sexual culture; each of us has made choices to sin. To varying degrees, each of us became ensnared by these choices, but we can overcome this affliction. Far too often, however, we ignore our own responsibility in this. We complain, "Well, of course I want to be free from impurity! I've been to the altar 433 times about it, haven't I? It just doesn't seem to be God's will to free me." 📖

*Discussion Questions*

A.  Fred resolved to make a covenant with his eyes, just as Job did in ancient times. Talk together about how guys can follow this example. Discuss all the obstacles that would have to be overcome.

B.  Pastor Jack Hayford came to a point of decision. Have you been there yet? If so, what encouragement or advice can you give the other guys? If you haven't reached this point, what do you think it will take to reach bottom?

C.  The authors point out that sex is everywhere—even in the church. Have you found this to be the case? Talk about it; how do you handle it in a way that is pleasing to God?

D.  Discuss what the authors mean by having a low-grade sexual fever (chapter 8). Then respond to the three bulleted questions they suggest a feverish guy should ask himself.

E.  How many in the group have prayed over and over again for deliverance from lust? What is the authors' answer to this situation? (Refer to the final six paragraphs of chapter 8).

# Steve's long slide

**This week's reading assignment:**

**chapter 9 of *Every Young Man's Battle***

*I must stress this important truth. If you base your life on wanting to feel good, any time something feels good, you'll believe it's acceptable. Every time there are no consequences, you'll believe that it's even more acceptable. It's so tempting to live that way! The world is always screaming at you to do what you want* when *you want. If it makes you feel the way you want to feel, then go ahead.*

*So I never delayed gratification. Feeling good was the ultimate goal of my life.*

—Steve Arterburn, from chapter 9 of *Every Young Man's Battle*

## EVERY YOUNG MAN'S TRUTH
*(Your Personal Journey into God's Word)*

As soon as you make a covenant with your eyes and begin to live authentic manhood, temptations will likely increase. What will you do? Will you be able to stand your ground? The Bible passages below can help. Invite the Lord to speak to your heart as you claim these scriptures for guidance and rely on His strength in the battles ahead.

So [Potiphar] left in Joseph's care everything he had…and
after a while his master's wife took notice of Joseph and said,
"Come to bed with me!"

But he refused…. "My master has withheld nothing
from me except you, because you are his wife. How then
could I do such a wicked thing and sin against God?" And
though she spoke to Joseph day after day, he refused to go
to bed with her or even be with her.

One day he went into the house to attend to his duties,
and none of the household servants was inside. She caught
him by his cloak and said, "Come to bed with me!" But he
left his cloak in her hand and ran out of the house.
(Genesis 39:6-12)

Count yourselves dead to sin but alive to God in Christ
Jesus. Therefore do not let sin reign in your mortal body
so that you obey its evil desires. Do not offer the parts of
your body to sin, as instruments of wickedness, but rather
offer yourselves to God, as those who have been brought
from death to life; and offer the parts of your body to him
as instruments of righteousness. For sin shall not be your
master, because you are not under law, but under grace.
(Romans 6:11-14)

His divine power has given us everything we need for life
and godliness through our knowledge of him who called us
by his own glory and goodness. (2 Peter 1:3)

1. What was the key to Joseph's success with sexual temptation? How would you apply this Bible passage to the temptations of pornography? lust? sex outside of marriage?

2. What does it mean that, as a believer, you are "dead to sin"? How does "offering yourself to God"—all the parts of your body—play a key role in making this a reality? Have you asked God how you can do this?

3. You have everything you need from God to resist temptation. So— what will you do the next time you are faced with sexual temptation?

☑ EVERY YOUNG MAN'S **CHOICE**
*(Questions for Personal Reflection and Examination)*

📖 While they were eight years older than I was, something happened when I found myself woven into the arms of these two roller-rink goddesses. I hadn't felt anything so intense, so magnificent since I walked down to the front of the church to accept Christ. 📖

📖 I had little to offer a girl, but I wanted everything from her. It didn't register with me that this was someone's future wife, or that she was a real human with real needs that I could meet. Instead, it was all about me and making me feel good. Had I been godly, she could have become *more* because of her relationship with me. Too often, she was *less* because I took from her only what a husband should take. 📖

4. Can you recall having an early experience like Steve's—when your sexuality was first awakened? What attitudes or patterns of behavior did that experience set in motion in your life?

5. What do you have to offer a young woman? Do you normally focus on what you have to give or—as Steve did—consider only what you can take?

6. What does it mean to help a girl become more rather than less because of her relationship with you? Are you willing, before God and the guys in your group, to make such a commitment?

### EVERY YOUNG MAN'S WALK
*(Your Guide to Personal Application)*

📖 Compromise is a killer that seems so innocent in the beginning. Yet when you compromise and do a small thing you know isn't right, it rarely stays small or ends there. It becomes easier and easier to choose the wrong path the next time around.

Then it feels as if the wrong path begins to choose you. 📖

📖 All I wanted to do was to feel good, and I had decided long ago that I was willing to compromise to feel good. 📖

📖 If you connect the dots of my life—the cheating, the compromise, the masturbation, the early exposure to pornography, the objectification of women, and the promiscuity—you end up with an abortion....

Examine the dots in your life. What picture forms behind you as you connect these dots on your walk to your future? 📖

7. Where do you find areas of killer compromise in your life these days? What steps do you need to take to stop the bleeding?

8. What are some of the destructive consequences of only wanting to feel good?

9. Take some time to connect the dots in your life so far. What patterns have they formed? Why?

10. Still thinking about your dots, consider: What kind of man do you want to become? Are the things you're doing today leading you to, or away from, that goal?

11. In quietness, review what you have written and learned in this week's study. If further thoughts or prayer requests come to your mind and heart, you may want to write them here.

12. What for you was the most meaningful concept or truth in this week's study? What do you believe God wants you to do in response?

13. How would you talk this over with God? Write your response here as a prayer to Him.

👦👦 EVERY YOUNG MAN'S TALK
*(Constructive Topics and Questions for Group Discussion)*

### Key Highlights from the Book to Read Aloud and Discuss

📖 I thought nothing could feel as good as becoming a Christian, but rolling around the rink with those two perfect "10s" was the discovery that there are some things in this world that can make a person feel *really* good. After that night, I decided I wanted to feel really good. And I decided that night to begin a search of all things that felt good. 📖

📖 When you learned to masturbate, you didn't learn how to commit the unpardonable sin. You didn't engage in some perversion or do what only mentally ill people do. You did what almost everyone learns to do. For a few, the practice is of little consequence, but for many, it becomes a destructive habit or dependency.

It certainly became a problem for me. 📖

📖 The relationship broke up, as is usually the case, but the abortion didn't buy me peace. A simple thought continued to haunt me mercilessly. I hadn't simply purchased an abortion—I had killed my own child! That so-called glob of tissue was bone of my bone and flesh of my flesh. I had it snuffed out. 📖

## Discussion Questions

A. Steve decided early in his life to search for what felt good. What are your reactions to this? Can you relate? Do you have a story to tell similar to Steve's roller-rink event?

B. Steve talks about not getting caught when cheating on a school test. How did that shape his future attitudes about sexual activity? What did he fail to realize in those early years?

C. How do you think Steve's grandfather's attitude toward pornography influenced Steve? Who, in your life, seems to have similar influence? How are you coping with that?

D. Consider Steve's thought (on the previous page) regarding masturbation. Is it true that it's of little consequence for some guys? How do you think the act become a self-destructive habit, as in Steve's case? What is your basic advice to other Christian guys about masturbation?

E. Steve's attitude about just feeling good eventually caused him great pain and loss. He even pushed a girl to get an abortion. How does his experience seem to fulfill what the Bible says in Galatians 6:8? What does this mean to you personally, and how would you apply it to your determination to live as God's man?

# the M word

**This week's reading assignment:**
**chapters 10–13 of *Every Young Man's Battle***

*Since God didn't address masturbation directly in Scripture, the questions can seem endless. Theologians will argue over this until Christ returns, and maybe that's how it should be whenever Scripture is silent. Even we coauthors have found it difficult to decide together what to label masturbation and where to draw the lines of sin.*

—from chapter 10 of *Every Young Man's Battle*

## EVERY YOUNG MAN'S **TRUTH**
*(Your Personal Journey into God's Word)*

The Bible passages below show an amazing contrast. In Romans 7, the apostle Paul wrote of his struggle with sin. He apparently had an ongoing battle with some kind of habit or addiction. Maybe he was too ashamed to name exactly what it was. But we do know that he felt powerless to overcome it by sheer willpower alone—until he found a way out *apart* from willpower, something he described in Romans 8.

So consider the role of willpower in your own life as you confront sexual temptation. First, feel Paul's pain in Romans 7. Surely you can relate to his sense of hopelessness as habitual sin threw him against the wall, time after time. Then move to Romans 8, and rejoice with Paul in his victory through Christ. Everything for him, and for you, depends on what is done with the mind. Is it given over to the sinful nature or to the Spirit of God?

> I do not understand what I do. For what I want to do I do not do, but what I hate I do. And if I do what I do not want to do, I agree that the law is good. As it is, it is no longer I myself who do it, but it is sin living in me. I know that nothing good lives in me, that is, in my sinful nature. For I have the desire to do what is good, but I cannot carry it out. For what I do is not the good I want to do; no, the evil I do not want to do—this I keep on doing. Now if I do what I do not want to do, it is no longer I who do it, but it is sin living in me that does it.
>
> So I find this law at work: When I want to do good, evil is right there with me.… What a wretched man I am! Who will rescue me from this body of death? (Romans 7:15-21,24)

> There is now no condemnation for those who are in Christ Jesus, because through Christ Jesus the law of the Spirit of life set me free from the law of sin and death. For what the law was powerless to do in that it was weakened by the sinful nature, God did by sending his own Son in the likeness of sinful man to be a sin offering. And so he condemned sin in sinful man, in order that the righteous requirements of the law might be fully met in us, who do not live according to the sinful nature but according to the Spirit.

Those who live according to the sinful nature have their minds set on what that nature desires; but those who live in accordance with the Spirit have their minds set on what the Spirit desires. The mind of sinful man is death, but the mind controlled by the Spirit is life and peace. (Romans 8:1-6)

1. Think about the habits in your life that you have tried and tried to overcome. When the great apostle Paul thought about his own sinful habits, he felt "wretched." Can you relate?

2. What does the passage in Romans 7 tell you about the strength of willpower? Why can't it break a sinful habit?

3. What awesome insight did the Lord give Paul in Romans 8? How does this apply to you when you face your destructive habits and addictions?

4. What is the key to overcoming the "law of sin and death"?

## ☑ EVERY YOUNG MAN'S CHOICE
*(Questions for Personal Reflection and Examination, Chapters 10 and 11)*

📖 What's so great with men I've worked with, who have been masturbating with pornography since they were teens, is that when they stop, they find there's a different world out there. They find that they can handle stress differently. When they go without masturbating for a month, they feel so clean and good about themselves. 📖

📖 When we masturbate, some of us come to our Father and say, "I've masturbated again, and I'm not worthy to be called Your son." He brushes that aside, saying, "No one but Jesus is *worthy* to be called My Son, but I love you and forgive you." He demonstrates that love by presenting us with a ring, robe, and shoes. Then He says, "In case you forgot, Jesus picked these up at Calvary for you. That makes you worthy enough for me. Now let's celebrate and enjoy each other!" 📖

5. How do you react to the statement that without masturbating, guys start feeling clean and good? Have you found this to be true in your own life? Why or why not?

6. What do the authors mean by saying that no one is worthy to be called God's son? How does their explanation help you when you're feeling guilty about falling to temptation?

## EVERY YOUNG MAN'S WALK
*(Your Guide to Personal Application, Chapters 10 and 11)*

> Many other issues besides family problems can prompt a young male to pleasure himself in order to mask the pain felt elsewhere in his life. Maybe a guy has acne problems or big ears or a lisp. Whatever. The point is, it doesn't do any good to pile a bucket-load of "You ain't no good" on top of him. Self-condemnation only sets the cycle of masturbation into a downward spiral, causing deeper embarrassment and humiliation.

📖 This is what God is most concerned with. You're already His son. What He wants now is for you to move back closer to Him. 📖

7. What self-esteem issues might cause Christian guys to masturbate? Would you be willing to cite an example from your own life that could help the others in your group? Have you noticed the "downward spiral" that the authors speak of?

8. Take a long, careful look at how masturbation may be affecting your relationship with God. What is required for you to move back closer to Him?

9. What for you was the most meaningful concept or truth in chapters 10 and 11? What do you believe God wants you to do in response?

10. How would you talk this over with God? Write your response here as a prayer to Him.

## 👥 EVERY YOUNG MAN'S TALK
*(Constructive Topics and Questions for Group Discussion, Chapters 10 and 11)*

### *Key Highlights from the Book to Read Aloud and Discuss*

> 📖 In the last analysis, splitting hairs over what we call masturbation is silly. There are only two questions that matter. If you're in bondage to masturbation, should you try to break free? The answer is yes. Is it possible to break free? We believe it is. 📖

> 📖 When we sin, God doesn't shout, "Hell and damnation on you!" Since we're saved, He knows full well that there's now no more condemnation for us because of Christ. Remember, He personally had the apostles write that into the Bible! Jesus paid it all. Our Father isn't interested in making us pay further by adding shame after another orgasmic failure in cyberspace.
>
> God, your Father, is *for* you. 📖

📖 We hope that thousands of readers of this book will decide to stop pouring gasoline on a hot fire of passion, desire, and lust. We're about to show you how, and we believe that those who take this path will never regret it. We don't expect anyone, after having applied the forthcoming advice, to later declare, "Gee, I just wish I had masturbated more." 📖

## *Discussion Questions for Chapters 10 and 11*

A. Which parts of these chapters were most helpful or encouraging to you? Why?

B. Talk about the themes the authors raise at the beginning of chapter 10 (pages 107-108). Where do you tend to land in your view of masturbation—is it sin or not?

C. Do you agree that the key question is not whether masturbation is sin but rather: "If you're in bondage to masturbation, should you try to break free"? Why or why not?

D. What does "Jesus paid it all" mean to you? Tell how this biblical truth can apply to a guy's struggles with lust—and with guilt.

E. How do guys tend to pour gasoline on their sexual desire? Do you believe this habit can be stopped? How?

F. Together, turn to the four requirements to stop masturbating offered at the end of chapter 11 (under "Being Free from Sexual Fevers"). Talk about the practical applications of each step. Discuss the difficulties a guy might face in putting these requirements into practice.

---

*Note: If you're following a twelve-week track,*
*save the rest of this lesson for the next session.*
*If you are on an eight-week track, keep going.*

---

## ☑ EVERY YOUNG MAN's CHOICE

*(Questions for Personal Reflection and Examination, Chapters 12 and 13)*

📖 Loneliness, insecurity, and broken family relationships are often the steppingstones to masturbation. We replace that lost intimacy with the false intimacy of masturbation. A close relationship with God and our friends will make the false intimacy of masturbation unnecessary. 📖

📖 Perhaps you've felt the same type of anger and pain in your family relationships. Such anger often opens a door to pornography and masturbation. The desire to become close to *somebody* can also drive you quickly into the arms of women or one-sided friendships. Rather than turn to God, you truly can begin looking for love in all the wrong places, hoping for something, anything, to take the place of that loss. 📖

11. Right now, prayerfully search your life: Where do you find loneliness? Insecurity? Broken relationships? Lost intimacy? What lost intimacy in your relationships do you tend to replace with masturbation?

12. Have you noticed that you tend to move toward pornography when you are angry, tired, hungry, or frustrated in some way? In what ways might you tend to "look for love in all the wrong places"? How have you felt inside, spiritually, when you've done so?

 EVERY YOUNG MAN'S **WALK**
*(Your Guide to Personal Application, Chapters 12 and 13)*

> &#x1F4D6; I'll never forget the day when I (Fred) came home from elementary school, tripping quickly down the school bus steps with my sisters and rushing into the house to eat cookies, then to go outdoors to play army and float boats down the creek. When we entered the house, however, my mother called the three of us into the living room to talk. She *never* did that, so I sensed that something serious had happened. &#x1F4D6;

> &#x1F4D6; Once you decide to starve Mr. Sex Drive, however, his weight and heft will shrink. He'll shed pounds overnight. All you have to do is stop feeding him the cable TV, videos, Internet, magazines, and fantasy. &#x1F4D6;

13. Think carefully about the impact his parents' divorce had on Fred. How did he react to his pain and loss? In what negative ways might you be reacting to pain and loss in your own life?

14. Why do you think inner pain and sexual desire are so related? How do you notice this in your actions?

15. What first step could you take to begin starving your sumo sex drive?

16. What for you was the most meaningful concept or truth in chapters 12 and 13? What do you believe God wants you to do in response?

17. How would you talk this over with God? Write your response here as a prayer to Him.

### EVERY YOUNG MAN'S **TALK**

*(Constructive Topics and Questions for Group Discussion, Chapters 12 and 13)*

### *Key Highlights from the Book to Read Aloud and Discuss*

📖 Another episode occurred when I was fourteen. Dad called Mom early one week and gave her the following order: "Have Freddie ready for me to pick up Friday night at seven o'clock. I've got a clean prostitute arranged for the evening. It's time for him to learn about love." He didn't understand why my mother and I were repulsed by the bizarre idea. 📖

📖 God turns to you and says, "Get into the ring." So you obey, but Mr. Sex Drive knocks you clean into the wall again.

Turning to God with pleading eyes, you cry, "See, God? Save me from this monster! Don't You love me?"

"Of course I love you," says the Creator of the universe. "Don't you love Me?"

"Lord, you know that I do!"

"Then starve the sumo!" 📖

&#x1F4D5; If you can't control your sex drive, whose fault is it? Is it God's, for giving you the sex drive? Or is it yours, because you've jumped on the gas pedal and sped past the red line far too often? &#x1F4D5;

## Discussion Questions for Chapters 12 and 13

G. What do you think Fred's father's prostitute arrangement would do in the heart of a young man? What problems did this cause for Fred?

H. Consider the benefit of forming accountability relationships. Together, read through the part in chapter 12 in which Ron checks up on Nathan (page 126). What do you think of this form of accountability? Would it work for you? Why or why not?

I. What does it really take to starve the sumo? Generate a list of practical actions guys can take to make this powerful wrestler lose weight.

J. Have you ever been tempted to blame God for your lack of sexual control? According to the authors, what is wrong with the logic behind that approach? What is the better way?

# setting your defenses

**This week's reading assignment:**

**chapters 14–17 of *Every Young Man's Battle***

*[Satan's] greatest attack weapon will be deception. He knows Jesus has already purchased your freedom. He also knows that once you understand how to starve Mr. Sex Drive, you'll probably push the big fellow right out of the ring in short order. So he deceives and confuses. He tricks you into thinking that you're a helpless victim. He tells you that sexual sin is just part of being a man and that there's nothing you can or should do about it. He tells you that you don't need to live a life of obedience because* obedience *is just another word for legalism.*

—from chapter 14 of *Every Young Man's Battle*

## EVERY YOUNG MAN'S TRUTH
*(Your Personal Journey into God's Word)*

The Bible passages below are excellent resources for spiritual battle and will help you set up your defenses as you fight for personal purity. Remember that this battle's basic strategy is simply to rely on the Lord, by faith, day by day. But that doesn't mean you have nothing to do! In response to God's goodness and power in your life, you are called to fill your eyes, your mind, and your heart with all that is good. In addition, you can take up your spiritual armor and fight off the subtle lies and temptations that are sure to hurtle your way. In other words, you have tremendous resources available for this fight; use them!

> I made a covenant with my eyes not to look lustfully at a girl. (Job 31:1)

> Be strong in the Lord and in his mighty power. Put on the full armor of God so that you can take your stand against the devil's schemes. For our struggle is not against flesh and blood, but against the rulers, against the authorities, against the powers of this dark world and against the spiritual forces of evil in the heavenly realms. Therefore put on the full armor of God, so that when the day of evil comes, you may be able to stand your ground, and after you have done everything, to stand. Stand firm then, with the belt of truth buckled around your waist, with the breastplate of righteousness in place, and with your feet fitted with the readiness that comes from the gospel of peace. In addition to all this, take up the shield of faith, with which you can extinguish all the flaming arrows of the evil one. Take the helmet of salvation and the sword of the Spirit, which is the word of God. And pray in the Spirit on all occasions with all kinds of prayers and requests. With this in mind, be alert and always keep on praying for all the saints. (Ephesians 6:10-18)

Flee from sexual immorality. All other sins a man commits are outside his body, but he who sins sexually sins against his own body. Do you not know that your body is a temple of the Holy Spirit, who is in you, whom you have received from God? You are not your own; you were bought at a price. Therefore honor God with your body (1 Corinthians 6:18-20)

1. How do you define "looking lustfully" at a girl? Answer thoughtfully and honestly: Does your definition allow you to rationalize an improper gaze or thought? Are you clear about the boundary lines you've promised God you will not cross?

2. Prayerfully study the pieces of spiritual armor laid out in Ephesians 6. Which do you most need today? (Suggestion: Imagine taking each piece into your hands. Then ask God to bless you as you put it on and use it.)

3. The passage in 1 Corinthians can act as a powerful shield against temptation. For example: How does it help you to recall that your body is where God's Spirit lives? And what impact does this idea have—that your body has been bought by the Lord?

☑ EVERY YOUNG MAN'S CHOICE

*(Questions for Personal Reflection and Examination, Chapters 14 and 15)*

📖 For teens and young adults, sexual gratification comes from three places: the eyes, the mind, and the body. Therefore, as in any war, you must blockade the "shipping lanes" of the eyes and mind that drive you toward sexual sin and that keep your enemy strong. 📖

📖 It may be useful to memorize several verses of Scripture about purity.… But in the cold-turkey, day-to-day fight against impurity, having several memory verses might be as cumbersome as strapping on a hundred-pound backpack to engage in hand-to-hand combat. You aren't agile enough to maneuver quickly.

That's why we recommend a single "attack verse," and it better be quick. 📖

4. How well have you been blockading the shipping lanes to your eyes and mind? What helps the most? What tends to mess you up?

5. Why is it best to have a quick-and-easy verse to recall when temptation hits?

6. What is your chosen attack verse? When did you last use it? How well did it work? (If you have not yet selected one, prayerfully choose one from the passages above and begin to commit it to memory this week.)

## EVERY YOUNG MAN'S WALK

*(Your Guide to Personal Application, Chapters 14 and 15)*

> There'll always be spiritual opposition. The enemy constantly whispers in your ear. He doesn't want you to win this fight, and he knows the lies that break down a young man's confidence and will to win. You can expect

to hear lies and plenty of them. Here's a list of some of
the all-time favorites… 📖

📖 Your first step is listing your own "greatest enemies."…
In choosing them, remember that they must be areas
from which you visually draw sexual satisfaction. 📖

7. Review Satan's lies (and the countering truths) found on page 144.
Which of these lies are you most often tempted to believe? What effect
have these lies had on your spiritual morale? How can you build up
your truth defenses in this area?

8. Take plenty of time to consider your personal greatest enemies. Then
respond to the authors' questions: What are the most obvious and pro-
lific sources of sensual images coming your way? Where do you look
most often? Where are you weakest?

9. Re-read the case of Derrick found on pages 156-157. What was his basic problem? Where have you, too, stepped outside your rights lately? How could you make a change for the better?

10. What for you was the most meaningful concept or truth in chapters 14 and 15? What do you believe God wants you to do in response?

11. How would you talk this over with God? Write your response here as a prayer to Him.

### EVERY YOUNG MAN'S **TALK**

*(Constructive Topics and Questions for Group Discussion, Chapters 14 and 15)*

### *Key Highlights from the Book to Read Aloud and Discuss*

> You want your heart to be right and your boundaries clear. To accomplish this, you need to build three perimeters of defense into your life:

1. You need to build a line of defense
   with your *eyes.*

2. You need to build a line of defense
   in your *mind.*

3. You need to build a line of defense
   in your *heart.* 📖

📖 I (Fred) had no problem coming up with a list of my
six biggest areas of weakness. Let me share how I dealt
with them... 📖

📖 Consider a specific example. I (Fred) recall once walking down a hotel hallway to the ice machine. On top of the
machine lay a *Playboy* magazine. Believing I had a right to
choose my behavior, I asked myself this question: *Should I
look at this* Playboy *or not?* 📖

*Discussion Questions for Chapters 14 and 15*

A. Which parts of these chapters were most helpful or encouraging to
   you, and why?

B. Of the three lines of defense you need, name the one that is strongest
   at this time in your life. Which is the weakest? Have the guys in your
   group suggest ways you can shore up this weak area.

C. The authors say that, with the habit of sexual impurity, the best
   method is not a gradual reduction. Instead, you must go cold turkey.
   Do you agree? Why or why not?

D. Take some time to let each guy talk about his own Six Biggest Areas of Weakness. Then discuss how effective Fred's methods of defense would be in your own life.

E. Ask some volunteers to talk about how they have been doing with their "eye covenant." Unite in prayer that each group member would be strong in his commitment.

F. Have a discussion about Fred's experience at the hotel with *Playboy*. What did you learn from Fred that you could add to your lines of defense in such situations?

G. At the end of chapter 15, Fred and Steve admit that maybe their plan sounds a little crazy. How do you respond to that? If you've been attempting to implement their plan, tell your group how it's going so far.

---

*Note: If you're following a twelve-week track,*
*save the rest of this lesson for the next session.*
*If you are on an eight-week track, keep going.*

---

## ☑ EVERY YOUNG MAN'S **CHOICE**
*(Questions for Personal Reflection and Examination, Chapters 16 and 17)*

&#x1F4D6; You have a flood on your hands, and that flood has to settle back into its banks. This means your sex drive has to dry up to normal levels as a drought of images and orgasms has its natural effect. That will take some time—probably more than three weeks. &#x1F4D6;

  It's so important to remember that God once looked upon His only begotten Son in Gethsemane as He struggled to submit in the biggest battle of His life. Jesus' submission was precious to the Father. Now this same Father is looking down from heaven upon you, His adopted son, as you struggle to submit in *your* battle for sexual purity. Sure, He wants victory, but…the very fact that you've entered the fray is precious to Him.  

12. Were you expecting a quick victory against sexual impurity? If so, how do you respond to the authors' warnings about slow-downs?

13. How does God view you these days? (Suggestion: Imagine being God for a moment; draw a picture of your adopted son in the space below. Label it with how you feel about this young man.)

### EVERY YOUNG MAN'S WALK
*(Your Guide to Personal Application, Chapters 16 and 17)*

  Another reason the process may slow down is that your commitment and discipline to this process of purity may take some time to kick in. Our society doesn't glorify discipline all that much, especially in high school. This means it may take you some time to learn a disciplined lifestyle. 📖

📖 Like the father in the prodigal son story, your heavenly Father is thrilled just to see you at the crest of the hill walking toward Him. If you stumble a bit as you come home, it won't change the fact that He is eagerly waiting for you to arrive. Just get up and get walking again. Reject discouragement and fall into His arms. 📖

14. How disciplined are you, in general? What about in the area of sexual purity? What is the next step for you?

15. How, exactly, could you plan to reject discouragement the next time you fail? Jot a plan.

16. The authors warn against viewing your sexuality as something shame-fully separate and distinct from you. What would help you remember that God gave you your body, your desires, and your sexuality?

17. What for you was the most meaningful concept or truth in chapters 16 and 17? What do you believe God wants you to do in response?

18. How would you talk this over with God? Write your response here as a prayer to Him.

## EVERY YOUNG MAN'S TALK
*(Constructive Topics and Questions for Group Discussion, Chapters 16 and 17)*

### Key Highlights from the Book to Read Aloud and Discuss

📖 *Eric says:* "Porn leaves a big hole of emptiness, but I can-not get myself to turn away from it when I'm the only one in my lonely apartment. I've tried bouncing my eyes, but that's as far as I can go. What happens after that is that I cannot concentrate on my work. I can't get anything done because sex constantly floods my preoccupations and thoughts." 📖

📖 While we're talking about discipline, let's go beyond our concern for our eyes. We must also be concerned with where we place ourselves in other ways. 📖

📖 For me (Steve) the most difficult part of this book is providing a standard for you that doesn't inflict needless shame but instead guides you toward a life of meaningful relationships and lays a foundation for your sexuality being fully integrated into your marriage relationship. 📖

### Discussion Questions for Chapters 16 and 17

H. Consider Eric's statement about pornography. If you were his best friend, what would you advise him to do?

I. David made this comment (page 163): "I'm sorry, but telling a man he should go at his wife with great gusto and then telling the single guy to wait for a nocturnal emission is insane!" Do you agree or disagree? Why?

J. Together, read through the experiences of Tim, Mike, Dave, and Josh in the last three paragraphs of chapter 17 (page 166). Talk about the places where you have trouble with increased temptation—and also talk about what has worked for you in winning this battle.

K. Take turns giving your reactions to this statement on page 169: "Don't view your sexuality as something shamefully separate and distinct from the rest of you."

L. The authors say that God knows what we're made of, and nothing surprises Him. What does this mean to you personally? In what ways does it encourage you?

M. Steve states that he wants to find a balance between (1) holding up a high standard for you to pursue, and (2) not piling on the guilt and shame. Do you think the authors have succeeded so far? Why or why not?

# from mustang to honor

**This week's reading assignment:**

**chapters 18–21 of _Every Young Man's Battle_**

_Can you control the mustang? Can you run him down on foot or simply wag your finger and admonish him? No, of course not.…_

_Your mind runs like a mustang. What's more, your mind "mates" where it wills with attractive, sensual girls. They're everywhere. With a mustang mind, how do you stop the running and the mating? With a corral around your mind._

—from chapter 19 of _Every Young Man's Battle_

### EVERY YOUNG MAN'S TRUTH
_(Your Personal Journey into God's Word)_

Before you begin this session, take some time to prepare your heart through Bible study. The passages below deal with a key aspect of successful Christian living—relying on the Holy Spirit. The great thing is, you do have an inner helper, the Spirit of God, living inside you. He wants you to succeed in your efforts to avoid impurity of any kind. If you let Him, the Spirit will give you the strength, in the midst of the most powerful temptations, to loosen your grip on lust, to ask yourself: _What do I really want?_, to just walk away.

I tell you the truth, anyone who has faith in me will do what I have been doing. He will do even greater things than these, because I am going to the Father. And I will do whatever you ask in my name, so that the Son may bring glory to the Father. You may ask me for anything in my name, and I will do it.

If you love me, you will obey what I command. And I will ask the Father, and he will give you another Counselor to be with you forever—the Spirit of truth. (John 14:12-17)

The Spirit helps us in our weakness. We do not know what we ought to pray for, but the Spirit himself intercedes for us with groans that words cannot express. And he who searches our hearts knows the mind of the Spirit, because the Spirit intercedes for the saints in accordance with God's will.…

And we know that in all things God works for the good of those who love him, who have been called according to his purpose. (Romans 8:26-28)

Flee from sexual immorality. All other sins a man commits are outside his body, but he who sins sexually sins against his own body. Do you not know that your body is a temple of the Holy Spirit, who is in you, whom you have received from God? You are not your own; you were bought at a price. Therefore honor God with your body. (1 Corinthians 6:18-20)

1. Why would Jesus call the Spirit a "Counselor"?

2. When have you most needed counsel from God's Spirit? Why not take a moment right now to ask Him for guidance?

3. Ever had difficulty praying? What awesome ministry does the Holy Spirit have for you when it comes to prayer?

4. Where does the Holy Spirit dwell? How does it make you feel to know that your body is a temple for Him?

☑ EVERY YOUNG MAN'S CHOICE

*(Questions for Personal Reflection and Examination, Chapters 18 and 19)*

📖 Every battle in life is hard, but with victory comes the spoils. So what are the "spoils" if you construct that perimeter around your eyes? Well, you're going to feel great about yourself, about your life, and about your future. 📖

📖 Currently, your brain moves nimbly to lust and to the little pleasure-high it brings. Your brain's worldview has always included lustful thinking. Double entendres, daydreams, and other creative forms of sexual thinking are approved pathways, so your mind feels free to run on these paths to pleasure. 📖

5. If you have been attempting to keep the covenant with your eyes, do you feel as if you've experienced some of the rewards—the spoils of victory? If so, take a moment to give thanks to God!

6. The authors explain that your mind is wild and will continue to lust as you seek to retrain it. How have you noticed this? What has been your usual response during the past week?

## 📓 EVERY YOUNG MAN'S WALK
*(Your Guide to Personal Application, Chapters 18 and 19)*

📖 Have you "lurked at your neighbor's door"?… This can easily refer to you as a young, single male. Lurking could mean stealing glances at her rack and rear. Lurking could mean roaming in areas you shouldn't be accessing on the World Wide Web. 📖

📖 There are young women you know who hit every attraction key on your keyboard—like Rachel, that new student, or maybe the new girl in the worship band who makes you breathless every time she gets up and sings. You neigh, drawing them toward your corral, but only in your mind.…

But you must lead her out of your corral and stop lurking. 📖

7. What forms of "lurking" seem to plague you the most?

8. When it comes to girls who hit your attraction key, what is your defense strategy? (Hint: Review the scripture attack verse you memorized a couple of sessions ago.) How well is it working?

9. What for you was the most meaningful concept or truth in chapters 18 and 19? What do you believe God wants you to do in response?

10. How would you talk this over with God? Write your response here as a prayer to Him.

## 👤👤 EVERY YOUNG MAN'S TALK

*(Constructive Topics and Questions for Group Discussion, Chapters 18 and 19)*

### Key Highlights from the Book to Read Aloud and Discuss

📖 Garrett began his story by noting that he was raised in the church, but by the time he was a senior in high school, he was drinking heavily, keeping a case of Bud longnecks iced up in a cooler that he kept in his trunk.... 📖

📖 There's nothing wrong with our attractions. Many of us have been lost in our attractions. You may be lost in one right now. I (Fred) got lost in high school with Julie. I noticed her early in my senior year, when Julie was a junior. 📖

&#x1F4D6; Don't you owe it to the Lord to put up a mental defense
perimeter? If not, you'll have a sad story to tell, like the one
we heard from Jake. He was the student leader of a youth
group, along with four others, including Gina. He was
standing strong and respected throughout the church. He
had no mental defense perimeter, however, because he bliss-
fully thought he didn't need one. As a result he allowed
Gina to come too close to his corral. &#x1F4D6;

## Discussion Questions for Chapters 18 and 19

A. Which parts of these chapters were most helpful or encouraging to
   you? Why?

B. Together, read back through the story of Garrett. What aspects of his
   experience ring a bell with you? Why? What good and bad decisions
   do you see him making?

C. Garrett reported that when he stayed close to the Word, it was easier
   for him to bounce his eyes. Have you noticed something similar in
   your own battle? Share your thoughts with the others in your group.

D. Review Fred's story about his so-called date with Julie (pages 185-
   187). Name some things that any guy can learn from this story.

E. Retrace the story of Jake's downfall (pages 189-190). What poor decisions did he make? What are the things Jake should have done?

---

*Note: If you're following a twelve-week track,*
*save the rest of this lesson for the next session.*
*If you are on an eight-week track, keep going.*

---

☑ EVERY YOUNG MAN'S CHOICE
*(Questions for Personal Reflection and Examination, Chapters 20 and 21)*

📖 I know you're my Christian brother, and I want to count on you to stand shoulder to shoulder with me in this call I have from God. Yes, I'm in my early forties and you may be in your teens or early twenties, but I'm as much your brother as your buddies are, and I'm counting on you not to lay your hands on my daughter just as much as your best friend is counting on you not to lay your hands on his girlfriend. Honor me in this. 📖

📖 Look at Uriah! He was so consumed by the purposes of God that he refused to go to his house even to wash his feet. His faithfulness and honor were so strong that, even when drunk, he didn't waver and wander on home for a little sack time with his own wife! Do you honor God's purposes like that? 📖

11. How does it feel to hear from a father regarding his daughter? Are you ready to honor Fred, Steve, and the other fathers of daughters you may date? What, exactly, does *honor* mean for you?

12. Review the Bible story of Uriah, described on pages 199-200. Have you ever been called to maintain the kind of discipline this man displayed? If so, how did you respond? If not, what do you think you would do in a future situation involving similar choices?

13. Amber spoke of the insecurity of many girls, which spurs them to give in to guys who are pushing for sexual intimacy. What would keep you from taking advantage of a girl like that?

### 👟 EVERY YOUNG MAN'S WALK
*(Your Guide to Personal Application, Chapters 20 and 21)*

> 📖 One of the biggest calls God has placed on *my* life is depending upon *your* character if you're alone with my Laura. That should make me uneasy, and it does. 📖

> 📖 Too often the only leadership we take is to charge across [a girl's] sexual boundaries. "Girls want guys to take the lead in the relationship," said Cassie. "Yet often it's the guys who are pushing the boundaries. When that has happened to me, I felt very resentful. I know that it makes girls just feel used. We neither feel validated in who we are nor in what we stand for as women." 📖

14. Imagine you're with Laura in a tempting situation. How much will you allow yourself to hear father Fred's words at that point? What would help you prepare in advance?

15. Why is it so important for the guy to take leadership in setting the sexual boundaries? (Suggestion: Think through exactly what your boundaries are going to be in the future. Be specific and detailed. Then ask the Lord to help you stick to your decision.)

16. The authors say, "It's not the act of defining sexual boundaries that makes you a spiritual leader. It's the act of defending them." Why is this distinction an important one?

17. What for you were the most meaningful concepts or truths in chapters 20 and 21? What do you believe God wants you to do in response to this week's study?

18. How would you talk this over with God? Write your response here as a prayer to Him.

👦👧 Every Young Man's TALK

*(Constructive Topics and Questions for Group Discussion, Chapters 20 and 21)*

## Key Highlights from the Book to Read Aloud and Discuss

    📖 Danny and Uriah are cut from the same cloth. Young men like Danny have real honor, courage, and love. 📖

    📖 The biggest difference is that sex is not a girl's priority in the relationship, and you need to understand this very clearly. Maybe it can most simply be said this way:

    • Guys give emotions so they can get sex.

    • Girls give sex so they can get the emotions.

    Guys, girls want a relationship with you, but they should not have to give sex to get it. 📖

## Discussion Questions for Chapters 20 and 21

F. Read aloud the first five paragraphs of chapter 20. What is your response to Fred's attitudes about his responsibilities in raising his daughter Laura? Imagine yourself the father of an attractive teenage daughter. Do you understand where Fred is coming from?

G. Discuss the various lines of defense Danny set for himself (pages 201-203). Evaluate each one based on how practical it would be for you to use. What do you like or dislike about each of Danny's decisions?

H. You may be saying, "Wait a minute. The girls I know sure look like they're all about sex." Is this really a true statement? Talk about it!

I. Discuss the differences in guys' and girls' attitudes toward sex in general. Do you agree that guys give emotions to get sex and girls give sex to get emotions? If so, what are some practical applications in your relationships with girls?

J. Toward the end of chapter 21, the question is raised: "How far can we go?" Discuss this together, taking into account everything you've learned so far in this study.

# ready for the challenge?

**This week's reading assignment:**

**chapters 22–23 of *Every Young Man's Battle***

*Amber is a twenty-year-old single woman at a Bible college. When I told her that I was writing this book…she said, "I wish I would have been told more specifically what 'sexual purity' really meant when I was growing up in the church. I was always taught that sexual purity meant 'no sexual intercourse,' but then I loved [your] definition: 'Sexual purity is receiving no sexual gratification from anything or anyone outside of your husband or wife.' That's a black-and-white definition that young people need to be taught. If you don't do anything else, please stress this definition."*

—Fred Stoeker, from chapter 22 of *Every Young Man's Battle*

📖 EVERY YOUNG MAN'S **TRUTH**
*(Your Personal Journey into God's Word)*

Congratulations! You've come to the final session in this study guide. We hope that you have learned, grown, and changed significantly during the past several weeks. We also hope that your relationship with God has deepened and that your sense of personal honor and integrity has generated a new level of peace and joy in your heart.

Before you launch into our final challenge to you, take a few moments to read and meditate on the following Bible passages, which focus on the theme of "Living by Faith." Take these words from God into your heart. And ask the Lord to make them real and practical to you as you continue to fight every young man's battle, day by day.

"O unbelieving generation," Jesus replied, "how long shall I stay with you? How long shall I put up with you? Bring the boy to me."

So they brought him. When the spirit saw Jesus, it immediately threw the boy into a convulsion. He fell to the ground and rolled around, foaming at the mouth.

Jesus asked the boy's father, "How long has he been like this?"

"From childhood," he answered. "It has often thrown him into fire or water to kill him. But if you can do anything, take pity on us and help us."

"'If you can'?" said Jesus. "Everything is possible for him who believes."

Immediately the boy's father exclaimed, "I do believe; help me overcome my unbelief!" (Mark 9:19-24)

The apostles said to the Lord, "Increase our faith!"

He replied, "If you have faith as small as a mustard seed, you can say to this mulberry tree, 'Be uprooted and planted in the sea,' and it will obey you. (Luke 17:5-6)

There was given me a thorn in my flesh, a messenger of Satan, to torment me. Three times I pleaded with the Lord to take it away from me. But he said to me, "My grace is sufficient for you, for my power is made perfect in weakness." Therefore I will boast all the more gladly about my weaknesses, so that Christ's power may rest on me. That is why, for Christ's sake, I delight in weaknesses, in insults, in hardships, in persecutions, in difficulties. For when I am weak, then I am strong. (2 Corinthians 12:7-10)

1. Mark tells us that Jesus healed a man's demon-possessed son. But Jesus seemed mildly offended by something the man said to him. What was it, and why do you think Jesus emphasized it?

2. If everything is possible for those who believe, what things (specifically, your thought life and your responses to temptation) are you believing God will do in your life in the year ahead? How much prayer are you devoting to these things? What commitment are you willing to make to improve your prayer life in this crucial area?

3. How much faith is required to do great things in God's kingdom? How much faith do you have at the moment?

4. The apostle Paul was frustrated by something in his life that just wouldn't go away. Do you think it may have been sexual desire or lust?

5. What was Paul's basic attitude toward his frustrating thorn in the flesh. What do you like about his view of how God uses our weaknesses?

## ☑ EVERY YOUNG MAN'S CHOICE
*(Questions for Personal Reflection and Examination)*

> 📖 We'd like to leave you with this challenge: We challenge you to live without premarital sex. We challenge you to live without masturbation. We challenge you to clean up what you're watching and the thoughts you're thinking. 📖

📖 Today, the sexual lines have been so blurred that no one knows what's right or wrong, holy or profane. To put it bluntly, you're living in the era of masturbation. There's more masturbation today and more things to masturbate over than ever before. There are entire industries centered on the practice of masturbation. The porn industry wants you to masturbate compulsively so it can sell you products. 📖

6. Think about the four challenges the authors give in the first quotation. For each one, consider: Am I ready to commit, without compromise?

7. Do you agree that you are living in the era of masturbation? If so, have you ever thought of yourself as a pawn, or victim, of the porn industry? How does this make you feel?

8. What new insights have you gained about homosexuality from reading chapter 23, which talks to guys who have homosexual desires?

9. How are the overall principles in this entire book just as applicable to a guy with homosexual desire? List a few of those basic principles that you can recall.

## 📖 EVERY YOUNG MAN'S WALK
*(Your Guide to Personal Application)*

📖 We challenge you to stop ridiculing your friends who are trying to walk closer to God. We challenge you to let the girls in your life know that you care more about their hearts than their bodies. 📖

📖 Thanks, Aaron, for sharing your incredible story. You decided that it was time, and you slew that monster of pornography. You changed the direction of your life, saved your marriage, and became a godly parent to your children. Now that's what we call a turnaround. What about you? Isn't it time? 📖

📖 The world will tell you [as a guy with homosexual desires] that you must act on your feelings—sexualize them—and only then will you feel whole. They'll tell you that while your family or church will reject you, you'll find completion in a world where homosexual sex is good and the attention you've always craved is available. You can listen to the world, or you can hear another voice that appears fainter but grows stronger every day. 📖

10. Steve and Fred give two more man-to-man challenges in the first excerpt above. Have you ever been guilty of ridiculing someone who was trying to hold to the highest standards of sexual purity? What about caring for a girl's heart more than for her body? (If these questions produce some guilt, ask for God's forgiveness and make amends to those you have wronged.)

11. Review the story of Aaron (pages 216-219). What one or two things about his story have the most impact on you? Why? What key truth have you learned from Aaron that can help you in your quest for sexual integrity?

12. What is your reaction to the study results of Dr. Robert Spitzer? Why do you think his views on homosexuality—based on scientific research—are so rarely heard in our society today?

13. According to the authors, what is the role of personal choice when it comes to homosexual temptation?

14. In quietness, review what you have written and learned in this week's study. If further thoughts or prayer requests come to your mind and heart, you may want to write them here.

15. What for you was the most meaningful concept or truth in this week's study? What do you believe God wants you to do in response?

16. How would you talk this over with God? Write your response here as a prayer to Him.

## 🙂🙃 EVERY YOUNG MAN'S TALK

*(Constructive Topics and Questions for Group Discussion)*

### *Key Highlights from the Book to Read Aloud and Discuss*

📖 When I told our youth pastor I was writing this book, I asked him whether there was anything he felt was absolutely critical to include. He pleaded, "Fred, they know they're going to fail. They don't have the spiritual strength to say no, and they know it. Show them how to have that strength!" 📖

📖 Porn-related Web sites are also an amazing success. While the dotcom industry is in a shambles with all sorts of Web sites going out of business, seventy thousand adult pay-for-porn sites are flourishing. Clearly, men want to masturbate, so businesses have sprung up to meet that need. For the rest of your life, you'll be bombarded with sensual television shows, horny movies, bra-and-panty ads in newspapers and magazines, and neighborhood strip joints. All of this is waiting out there for you *because men have sought out intensity rather than intimacy in their sexuality.* 📖

📖 How many of us are like Elijah? I don't have an answer, but I do know this: God wants to use you to change these days.

We'll leave you with an inspirational story of a unique young man named Aaron, a person whom God is using in these special days... 📖

*Discussion Questions*

A. Do you agree with the youth pastor's belief that young men "know they're going to fail"? Do you believe God has given you strength to live in sexual purity? If so, tell how.

B. Why do you think the intensity of this false intimacy of masturbation is so tempting when appropriate, real interpersonal intimacy is available?

C. How do you guys handle the temptation to go to porn Web sites? What advice can you give other guys about this?

D. Together, let's review the story of Aaron. What key truths should we learn from his experiences?

E. Briefly summarize the authors' explanation of homosexual development. Does it make sense to you? Why or why not?

F. What is your reaction to the research results of Dr. Robert Spitzer? What encouragement is there in his words for any guy who has homosexual desires?

G. Before we bring our session to an end, let's take a moment to reflect on what we've studied and discussed over the previous weeks.

   • What do you want to thank God for as a result of this study?

- What do you sense God most wants you to understand at this time about your sexuality and purity?

- In what specific ways do you believe He now wants you to more fully trust and obey Him?

# don't keep it to yourself

If you've just completed the *Every Young Man's Battle Workbook* on your own and you found it to be a helpful and valuable experience, we encourage you to consider organizing a group of guys and helping lead them through the book and workbook together.

You'll find more information about starting such a group in the section titled "Questions You May Have About This Workbook."

# about the authors

**Stephen Arterburn** is coauthor of the best-selling Every Man series. He is founder and chairman of New Life Clinics, host of the daily "New Life Live!" national radio program, creator of the Women of Faith Conferences, a nationally known speaker and licensed minister, and the author of more than forty books. He lives with his family in Laguna Beach, California. Steve can be reached by e-mail at sarterburn@newlife.com.

**Fred Stoeker** is the founder of Living True Resources, whose mission is "to practically elucidate God's truth, encouraging and equipping men and women to rise up and *be* Christian, rather than to *seem* Christian." Fred is a best-selling author and conference speaker. He speaks to men about the subject of sexual purity and has counseled hundreds of couples in how to connect in intimate relationships with their spouses. Fred and his wife, Brenda, live in the Des Moines, Iowa, area with their four children. Fred can be reached by e-mail at fred@stoekergroup.com.

**Mike Yorkey** is the author, coauthor, or general editor of more than thirty books, including all the books in the Every Man series. He and his wife, Nicole, are the parents of two college-age children and live in Encinitas, California.

 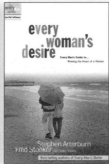  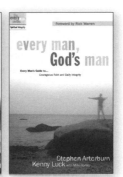

# every man's battle workshops

## from New Life Ministries

**n**ew Life Ministries receives hundreds of calls every month from Christian men who are struggling to stay pure in the midst of daily challenges to their sexual integrity and from pastors who are looking for guidance in how to keep fragile marriages from falling apart all around them.

As part of our commitment to equip individuals to win these battles, New Life Ministries has developed biblically based workshops directly geared to answer these needs. These workshops are held several times per year around the country.

- Our workshops **for men** are structured to equip men with the tools necessary to maintain sexual integrity and enjoy healthy, productive relationships.

- Our workshops **for church leaders** are targeted to help pastors and men's ministry leaders develop programs to help families being attacked by this destructive addiction.

---

### Some comments from previous workshop attendees:

*"An awesome, life-changing experience. Awesome teaching, teacher, content and program."* —DAVE

*"God has truly worked a great work in me since the EMB workshop. I am fully confident that with God's help, I will be restored in my ministry position. Thank you for your concern. I realize that this is a battle, but I now have the weapons of warfare as mentioned in Ephesians 6:10, and I am using them to gain victory!"* —KEN

*"It's great to have a workshop you can confidently recommend to anyone without hesitation, knowing that it is truly life changing. Your labors are not in vain!"* —DR. BRAD STENBERG, Pasadena, CA

---

If sexual temptation is threatening your marriage or your church, please call **1-800-NEW-LIFE** to speak with one of our specialists.